I Love You Forever

An Exquisite Collection of the Loving Poems by Rumi

An Authentic Translation by:
S. Morteza Lajevardi

Peace and Love Institute

Published by Peace and Love Institute
www.PeaceAndLoveInstitute.com
First edition, 2023

ISBN: 978-1-7390764-6-7
E-book ISBN: 978-1-7390764-4-3
Hardcover ISBN: 978-1-7390764-5-0

Dedicated to the Infinite Love

Contents

Introduction

While the breeze on a beautiful day at the beginning of October caresses my face and body, I am pleased to introduce to you an exquisite collection of the best poems by Rumi. Following the publication of *The Garden of Persian Poetry* and after studying over 190 prominent poets during 1,000 years of Persian literature, I realized that Rumi was the happiest poet among them based on their works.

When you read the biography of Rumi, you'll find a gentleman who lived a beautiful and happy life in one of the most devastating eras in human history due to Mongolian attacks. In his massive collection of poetry, I found Rumi to be very positive, optimistic, and hopeful.

Jalaludin Muhammad Rumi was born in 1207 in Balkh, in eastern Persia and, when he was still a child, immigrated with his family to Konya, in eastern Anatolia.

His father was a prominent Islamic scholar and had many students; following his death, Rumi, at a young age, became his successor, teaching and preaching to his followers.

Rumi lived a normal life until he met Shams, an unknown mystic who flamed the Divine Love in Rumi's soul.

After his encounter with Shams, Rumi left all his social status and began his inner journey toward Truth.

Rumi's poetry reflects his spiritual journey. He never wrote his poetry but verbally expressed his inner world spontaneously while some of his followers were ready to write what he expressed. Rumi's poems are the eruption of his inner world.

The melody in Rumi's poetry is beautiful and exuberant. His followers danced (Sama dance or Sufi whirling) with the recitation of Rumi's poetry.

In my style of translation, I try my best to stay faithful to the original poems with minimal modifications. This allows readers to better ponder what the poet actually wanted to express rather than my interpretation.

When Rumi passed away, people from all religions in Konya participated in his funeral and cherished him.

The purity of Rumi's soul has been expressed in his poems, and after centuries they are still an illuminating light to promote peace, love, happiness, and acceptance in the world.

I Love You Forever is an expression of *Divine Love* to you.

All the best,
S. Morteza Lajevardi

Your Love

O Whose soul has raised my soul's
consciousness!
Each moment, your thoughts are
influencing my being.
Whatever you think and remember, at the
same moment, is passing through my
mind.
My soul is busy with your manners and
coquettishness while your trick is secretly
doing something different.
In memory of your lips, every morning, the
reed whines;
Your love has filled the mouth of the reed
with sugar and sweets.
For your moon-like face, stature, and
waistline, my soul is shining like the new
moon.
In the hope of you showing up,
I have made myself like the waist;
However, your eyes are looking at me with
rage.
You are looking at me with a temper,
Turning my heart upside down,
So that my ruined heart emigrates from
self.[1]

---

[1] Ego

There is a different equanimity in the session of lovers; the wine[2] of love makes another hangover.
Learning knowledge in school is a different work, yet love has a different world.

As I knew that love is my attachment and that the thousand-knot plait is on my hand,
Even though last night I was drunk with wine, today I am such that the wine is drunk with me.

That Eminency and Beauty Who is shining on the world and that Hidden Face Who is the Happiness Day;
As He is with us today,
We are all accompanying Him.
Last night and the night before last night are gone; the day is today.

[2] Divine love

The Light of Heart

The light of our heart: your beautiful face;
Our wings and feathers: your good temper.
Our feast is your laughing;
Our musk and flower scent are from your good fragrance.
O One for Whom our horoscope is your full moon!
Our shade is your pretty hair.
Our prayer mat is your gate soil;
Our arena is your good alley.
My heart doesn't move toward others,
As it is moving in your good direction.
If my heart goes toward others,
Your good shelter pulls it back toward you.
O, our drunkenness is for your Being!
We are floating in your good stream.
Being next to you, my silver has turned into gold.
I have become one for your unique goodness.
In your polo game, I place my head on your good ball; why shouldn't I?
I become silent;
As for longing for your goodness,
My commotion has disappeared.

Upon storing your love in my heart, I
burned everything, but your love.
I put aside reason, book, and competition
and learned to say poetry, sonnet, and
couplet.

For your grace, no servant is disappointed;
What is accepted by you is eternal.
To which particle did your grace shine and
it didn't become better than a thousand
suns?

Who is the Sun to compete with your face?
Who is the light-headed wind to reach your
hair?
The intellect, being the dignitary of the city
of being, goes crazy upon arriving in your
alley.

In the Eternal Paradise

Happy moments when we are sitting on the porch, *me* and *you*.
In two figures and two faces but in one soul, *me* and *you*.
At that moment, when *I* and *you* enter the garden, the water of life gives harmony to the garden and life to the birds.
At that moment, the stars of the galaxy come to watch us;
Me and *you* come together with verve without *I* and *you*.
The parrots of the sky all become sugar-eaters, in a state where we laugh at, *me* and *you*.
This is more incredible: *me* and *you* are here in the corner, but at the same time,
We are in Iraq and Khorasan, *me* and *you*.
In one image we are here on the Earth,
In another image,
We are in the eternal paradise,
Me and *you*.

They say there will be a supreme paradise
with pure wine and nymphs.
So, we keep the wine and Beloved in our
hands, as the end will be the same.

Lovelorn for your plait, people's condition
in paradise is a shame.
It's like being taken to the plain of heaven
but your heart feels tightened.

Enter the garden but don't look at the
greens;
At flower shops, don't look in each corner.
The flower laughs, saying to nightingales,
"Be silent but don't look at the silent ones."

Raising Your Sunshine

I am you; you are me; O friend! Don't go away.
Don't think of me as someone else,
And don't drive me away from your door.
Don't get lost in your endless temptation;
So that I don't hit my head unfairly like a wanderer.
The one who isn't separated from you, like a shadow, is me;
Don't stab your shadow. O friend!
O tree that casts thousands of shadows in every direction!
Caress the shadows and don't cut them off from your gem.
Hide all the shadows and annihilate them in the light;
Raise your sunshine and show your luminous face.
The king of the heart is bewildered by your hesitancy.
"Wisdom is the crown," said Ali[3] in an allegory.
Endow the crown with a new gem from your treasury.

---

[3] Prophet Muhammad's successor

The nightingale came to the garden,
And we were freed from the raven.
O darling! We come to the garden with you.
Like a lily and a flower, let's come out of ourselves;
Like flowing water, we go from one garden to another garden.

As long as I have wanted, I have asked for you from you.
With your love, I have embellished the love table.
I had a dream last night, but I forgot;
However, I know that I woke up drunk.

In the desire of Beloved, we are revolving;
God knows how we are in this welkin.
We wonder why the wise are alert;
And they wonder why we are crazy.

In the Circle of Lovers

Love is to fly in the sky,
Tearing off a hundred curtains with every breath.
First disconnecting each breath from the other and intersecting each step from the other;
Ignoring this world and seeing oneself.
I said, "O heart! Congratulations on arriving in the circle of lovers!"
Watching from the other side of perception and running in the alley of chests.
O heart! Where did you get this breath?
O heart! Where does your beating come from?
O bird! Speak with the language of birds.
I know the secret of understanding you.
Heart said, "I was at home working;
I flew to the home of water and flowers.
I left the house of creation so that I could create the house of creation."
Exhausted, they pulled me down.
Are you grabbing my face because I talk?

We are beautiful; beautify yourself.
Accustom yourself to us and forget others.
Do you want to be a mine of gems?
Open your heart and let your chest be the sea.

Do you know what the night is?
O wise sage! Listen;
Empty the circle of lovers from every stranger.
Especially tonight,
As Dignitary is in the house,
I am drunk, the moon is in love,
And the night is crazy.

I was a hermit; you made me a singer, head of banquet, and drinker.
I was sitting on my prayer mat;
I had dignity;
You made me a toy in the hands of children in the alley.

Where the Best City Is

Said a beloved to a lover, "O gentleman!
You have visited and roved many cities;
Which one was the best?"
He said, "The city where your beloved resides."
Wherever our king stands is the plain, even if it is a needle hole.
Wherever Joseph is, like a moon, is paradise, even if it is the bottom of a pit.

If you are searching for the house of the soul, you are soulful.
If you are searching for a morsel of bread, you are bread.
You are wise if you know this secret:
You are what you are searching for.

If I am not good, anyway, I worship Goodness.
If I am not wine, anyway, I am drunk with wine.
If I am not among prayers, anyway, I am a member of your tavern.[4]

Rise and go to stand before Goodness;
Talk with the affectionate Beloved.
Get out of this trap and enter Beloved's trap;
If He drives you away from His gate, enter from the roof.

---

[4] Spiritual encounters

The Rise of Soul

As the flower fell, the fruit began to grow.
As the body broke, the soul rose.
The fruit is the meaning and the blossom is the face.
The blossom is the good news and the fruit is the blessing.
As the blossom fell, the fruit appeared.
As this was diminishing, the other was increasing.
Unless bread is eaten,
How does it give strength?
Unless the wheat cluster is broken,
What can it give?
Unless a spice is not broken,
How can it increase the flavor?

Originally, my soul and yours were one;
The apparent side of mine and yours, and
the hidden side of mine and yours.
Saying mine and yours is naivety.
You and *I* have been removed between
you and *I*.

A love in perfection and charm in beauty;
The heart is speaking while the tongue is
speechless.
What would be rarer than this?
I am thirsty, whereas before me the pure
water is flowing.

On the path toward a desire, maturity is
necessary;
One should stretch out from the world.
Cure oneself of blindness,
As the whole world is He,
But conscious eyes are needed.

The Sea of Love

The Moon, about whom firmament couldn't even dream, returned.
He brought a fire that no water could quench.
Look at the house of my body and my soul;
For the cup of His love, my soul is drunk and the house is ruined.
As the Head of the tavern has become my heart's friend,
For His love, my blood becomes the wine and my heart is burning.
As my eyes are filled with His imagination,
A call is heard: O cup! Well done! O wine! Bravo!
Unawares, my heart saw the sea of love.
Part of me jumped into the sea, saying, "Find me!"
The sunny face, honor of Tabriz, and the light of the path;
Hearts are running forward like clouds in the sky.

O heart! They won't let you on the path with turmoil.
They won't let you reunite but in annihilation.[5]
Where birds are flying, until you have your own feathers and wings, they won't give you new feathers and wings.

O Friend! I am your companion;
Wherever you step in, I am your soil.
In the religion of love, how is it permissible to see your world, not you?

The ship is passing through the ocean, deeming nothing has passed.
We are passing through this world all the time, thinking the world is passing.

[5] Annihilation of ego

Love Explains

Love is evident in the wailing of the heart;
There is no disease like the sickness of the heart.
The cause of love is different from all other causes;
Love is the astrolabe[6] of God's secrets.
Being in love is superior to anything,
Leading us toward our destination.
Whatever I say to describe and express love,
When falling in love, I become ashamed of my description.
Although the articulation of the tongue is to enlighten, love without words is clearer.
As the pen was in a hurry to write,
When it wanted to write about love, it broke.
In the explanation of love, the intellect was stuck in the mud,
So love explained both love and falling in love.
The Sun became the reason for the Sun.
If you have a reason, don't ignore it.

---

[6] An ancient astronomical instrument

No one could know the King's Majesty
unless becoming an insane lover on the
way home.
Crazy is one who sees your face once,
Then, despite being far from you, has not
yet become insane.

Branches of trees are picking fresh flowers,
Seeing inside themselves the mine of the
gem.
Though trees might not have leaves,
Until they are standing,
They don't despair or give up.

If you become the prey of God, you will be
saved from sorrow;
If you go on your own, you will be stuck.
Know that your *self* is an obstacle on your
path;
Don't be the companion of *self*, as you
become weary.

Last night, while in love and keen,
I was begging Tapster for wine.
As He showed me His beauty and glory,
I became nothing whereas Tapster remained.

Your soul is eternal; your inner world is beautiful;
You are from that glory; you are from the light of God.
You are still unseen; what have you seen of your beauty?
At dawn, like a sun, you will rise inside yourself.

You are sugar! Scatter sugar because you are the sweetness of sugar.
Play the flute of fortune because you are melodious.

Aiming for Annihilation

O my restless heart! Tell the truth;
What a gem! Are you fire or water?
Are you a human or an angel?
Where have you come from and what kind of food have you eaten?
What have you seen in annihilation?
Why are you flying toward annihilation?
Why are you rooting me out?
Why are you aiming for annihilation?
You are the bandit of reason, tearing off your veil;
Every creature is wary of annihilation,
Except you, taking your belongings to annihilation.
You are going with ardor and in a hurry;
Drunk and ruined.
Not listening to any advice, you are carefree about people's coquettishness.
Like a flood, you are flowing from the mountain of the world toward the placeless ocean, smoother than my breath.
O wayward garden and spring!
Why are you blowing like a breeze!?

Your drunk lily and cedar;
What a flower! What an elegance!
Though among people, I ran away from everyone.
Gold in the mine has no value unless it is found and separated from impurity.

Have you seen a lover satiated by this craziness?
Have you seen a fish satiated in this ocean?
Have you seen a painting running away from the painter?
Have you seen an infatuated one asking a beloved for another beloved?

If fire sees you, it will sit in the corner, tamed.
In such a way, everybody picking flowers in the fire gets a bouquet.
This world without you is a torment,
May there never be a time without you.
I swear to your soul, a soul without you is in torture and woe.

You are the Ocean and I am the fish,
I am however you want.
Bless me; reign,
I am left alone without you.

Dancing for Happiness

As you show your flower-color face,
You make the stone dance for happiness.
Unveil your face another time;
Let lovers hear your voice;
So that knowledge loses its way,
And the wise breaks the custom;
So that water turns into a gem for your
image;
So that fire leaves the battle.
With your goodness, I don't want even the
Moon;
Neither those few earthly extinguishing
pendulums.
With your face, I don't talk about the
mirror or the rusted old sky.
You blew again and recreated another
form of this world.
In longing for His Mars-like eyes, O Venus!
Play the music again with the harp.

Be silent to hear the revelations from Truth;
As there are a hundred thousand lives in a clear revelation.

Where is Tapster of the soul to stir us up?
Let the thoughts of yesterday and tomorrow go away from our hearts.

More wondrous! People are flying like butterflies while you don’t see the Candle of hearts.
O our eyes! What crime did you commit that you are closed?
Let it go, repent, and leave the faults.

The Joy of Love

I said to my heart,
"Why are you like this?
How long are you going to stay with love?"
Heart said,
"Why don't you join us to enjoy the
pleasure of love?"
When you become conscious of the water
of life,
How would you choose anything else but
the fire of love?
O Whose delicacy is like a spirited wind!
Like water, you are the soul of figures,
And you are trustworthy for the mirror of
goodness.
A stingy person deems you miserly.
Though you seem an earthly being,
You are the soul of heaven.
Although on the ground,
You are the kohl for the eyes of certainty.
O ruby! You are from which mine?
Come into the circle; you are such a
beautiful jewel.

O the fame of the Moon! I am from you;
Look at me and yourself.
For your laughing, I have become a laughing flower garden.

Be like chess, silent in spirit but its presence is all tongue;
For the beauty of the king of the universe,
I am mellifluous and auspicious.

The new fortune said,
“Don’t walk and don’t bother;
I am coming to you with kindness and grace.”

As I am drunk with your face,
O wise sage!
Look at me with those drunk eyes.
My crazy heart is twisted by your drunk eyes;
Craziness and drunkenness are alike.
Look at my ruined heart optimistically
As the sun of an optimistic look rehabilitates the ruin.
Look at me once;
With that look, the wondrous trees appear from a seed.

I made a new promise last night;
I swore to your soul to keep my eyes on you;
I don't turn away from you even if you stab me with a blade;
I don't seek treatment from anyone else because my lovelornness is for your parting.
If you enter me into the fire,
I sigh but stay alive.
On your way, I rose like a speck of dust;
However, I will return to the soil of your path.

In falling in love with Friend, sacrifice reason.

If a mishap has covered your sky like a black night,
Eventually, that will direct you to the light.
Even if a mishap tries to kill you a hundred times,
In the end, it heals and revives you.

Sell cleverness and buy astonishment.
Cleverness is a suspicion but astonishment is consciousness.

Come in all, like butterflies;
Come in this grace where there are a hundred springs.

As you are not gaining anything by cunning, abandon cunning so that fortune comes to you.

Be silent, not sad;
A soul in love won't be vicious.

I was a particle, you raised me higher than a mountain;
I was lagging, you made me a harbinger.
You healed my ruined heart and purified me;
You made me drunk, and I clapped for myself.

Love is the garden of the heart, a land for fostering friends.
Love makes your soul blossom and green like a tree.
Love is fresh and happy, and its aspirant is fresher.
The figure of the world is old, and whoever is in love with it is older than that.

My soul and yours have been sewn together by fate;
I am happy, happy, happy before you;
O King of happy ones!

The Candle of Heart

From two thousand *I* inside me,
Oh wow! Who am I?
Listen to my cry; don't put your hand on my mouth.
As I am lost, don't spread shards on my path;
I will break whatever I find, whether you throw it or me.
With every breath, my heart was drunk with the thought of you;
If you are happy, I am happy;
If you are sad, I am sad.
If you are bitter, I become bitterness;
If you are kind, I become kindness.
O Beloved with sweet lips and beautiful chin! Being with you is happiness.
You are Principle; who am I? A mirror on your palm;
I become whatever you show, I am the testing mirror.
Your attributes are like cedar and greenery; my attributes are your shadow;
As I became the shadow of the Flower, I pitched my tent next to the Flower.

Without you, if I pick a flower, it turns into
a thorn in my palm;
With you, all my thorns turn into flowers
and jasmine.
Moment by moment, I pour the wine of the
lovelorn heart;
With every breath, I break my jug at the
Butler's door.
With every breath, I grab the collar of an
idol so that it scratches my face and rends
my shirt.
The kindness of Salah[7] of heart and path is
woven within my heart;
He is the candle of heart in the world; who
am I?
His candlestick.

[7] One of the close spiritual companions of Rumi

Where do I come from?
Where does the moral come from?
Butler! Serve the wine in the reviving cup;
Pour it on the soul.
Place the cup of soul in my hand;
O Helper of lovers!
May it be far from the lips of strangers;
Butler! Pour the wine.

Get up, O butler!, O enemy of shame and modesty! Come so that our fortune smiles; come smiling.

I am in love with the art of craziness;
I am fed up with culture and wisdom.

Happy in Love

Another time, the tune of the fortunate reed is heard;
O, soul! Dance; O, heart! Frolic.
The shining gem has made the world smile;
The reciting is beautiful;
The calling is heard.
The fragrance of the new spring, on the green field, happy in love, we are drunk and exulting.
He is the Ocean; we are the cloud;
He is the Treasure; we are the ruin;
We are particles floating in the sunlight.
Rebellious but forgiven, let me profess;
I split the Moon with the light of Mustafa[8].

[8] Prophet Muhammad

O, friends! Beloved has closed the escape paths;
We are lame gazelles; He is the Hunting Lion.
Is there any remedy other than surrender and consent?

Like the Sun, He doesn't sleep or eat;
He makes souls sleepless and having no need to eat.
Come and stay with me;
Be my companion so that in emanation you see my face.

For the ears of the thirsty, I am the sound of water, falling from the sky like rain.

Drunk with Wind Sound

O lovers, O lovers! Today, we are together;
Fallen in a flood to know ourselves.
If the flood covers the world with huge waves,
What sorrow do seabirds have?
With happy faces for the sweetness,
We learn from the sea and waves,
As the sea and storm give life to fish.
O sheik! Give us a towel and let us sink in the water;
O Moses! Come and cane the water with your wand.
This wind in everybody's head is devising a different plan;
The infatuation with Butler for me,
And everything else for you.
Yesterday, Butler was in the way of drunkards;
Today, He is pouring the wine for us, making us take off our cloaks.
You are the honor of the Moon and Jupiter;
You are hidden like a fairy;
You are mirthfully bringing us with you.
Won't you tell us where?

Everywhere you go, you are with me;
O Light of my eyes!
As you wish,
Either make me drunk or annihilate me.
Perceive the world as Mount Sinai and us as seekers like Moses;
Every moment, Truth is expressed in the mountain and splits it.
A part becomes greenery, another part becomes jasmine; some becomes a gem, and the remaining part becomes ruby and amber.
O seeker of meeting Him! Look at this mountain chain.
O mountain! What wind is passing through you? We are drunk with wind sound.
O gardener! O gardener! What have you wrapped us in?
If we have taken your grapes, you have taken our wineskin!

My Venus is moving in the firmament in a
different way;
In hearts and eyes, it is passing with
esteem.

On the night of your plait, the heart saw
your face as it would see in the day.
Like dawn, the night and day of Beloved
stealthily pass.

The spike-like eyebrow is unaware of His
moon;
If it is aware, why is it going beyond the
moon?

Hurrah Love!

Hurrah love! Hurrah love! That we have God;
How marvelous, how good, and how beautiful it is, O God!
How warm we are, how warm we are from this love like the sun.
How hidden, how hidden, and how visible it is, O God!
Hurrah Moon! Hurrah Moon!
Hurrah comrade wine! Who adorned the soul and the universe.
Hurrah ecstasy! Hurrah ecstasy! That has made the world excited;
Hurrah affair! Hurrah infatuation! Where God is.
Hurrah firmament! Hurrah firmament! God arises.
As we didn't crawl, we fell, not knowing what the uproar was for.
In every alley, there is a different kind of smoke; Again and again, what a craziness, O God!
No trap, no chain; why are we all chained? What is the confinement for? What is the chain for? O God!

What an image! What an image appears
on the canvas of the heart!
Wondrous! Wondrous! It is from heaven.
Be silent! Be silent! So that your secret isn't
disclosed;
As strangers are everywhere.

Every fresh seedling is brought to the
garden;
But dried ones, like firewood, are under the
axe.
In every moment, like a fresh seedling,
drink the water of meaning;
Give thanks for the flowing of the sugar
river in the love garden.

Look at me;
If you look at anything else but me,
certainly you are unaware of God's love.
Look at a face flavored with Truth;
May you abruptly become fortunate from
that face.

If your heart is connected to heaven, talk;
Don't be afraid of becoming empty.

Without *We*

We began a journey, without *we*;
There, He opened our hearts, without *we*.
The Moon, always being hidden from us,
put His face on our face, without *we*.
As we sacrifice our souls in love of Friend;
He removed our sorrow, without *we*.
We are always drunk without drinking
wine;
We are always happy, without *we*.
Don't ever remember us;
As we are ourselves the remembrance
without *we*.
We have become without *we*, saying
mirthfully:
May we always be without *we*.
All doors were closed on us;
He opened the door and let us in, without
we.
The king is our servant, without *we*.
We are freed from good and bad, freed
from obedience and corruption, without
we.

Thank God for seeing your face;
Suddenly, I found a way toward you.

You threw a quest in my heart so that I enter your river in search of you.

As He is working on my affairs, why should I try other ways?
As I have tasted His lips, why should I think of sugar?

The Magical Breath

O coadjutors! Go and bring our friend, the truant beloved, to me.
With sweet lyrics and ornated pardons,
Bring back to home the good moon, the handsome.
If he promises, “I’ll come a little bit later,” don’t listen;
All his promises are deceitful;
He is deceiving you.
With his warm, magical breath, he ties the water and blocks the wind.
With happy greetings, when my beloved comes, sit down and watch the wonders of God.
When his beauty shines, how scant would be the beauty of good ones;
The sun of his face erases all other lights.
O, lively heart! Go to Yemen, say greetings, and favor the priceless agate.

Though I am drinking wine, I am still
conscious;
Why should I rummage through the
heavenly session?
I am a devotee of such a beautiful Moon;
Why should I leave Beloved and follow
every astrologer's saying?

On the top of the seventh heaven, why
should I say the name of the Earth?
I am the zeal of every angel; why should I
mention mankind?

Take our hands; buy us;
Remove the curtain, but don't decry us.

Come Back Home

Among lovers, don't be canny;
The ruby cassock is special for love.
May the wise be far away from lovers!
May malodor be far away from the zephyr.
When reason comes,
say, "There is no way";
When a lover comes,
Say a hundred hurrahs.
In the time of sacrifice, reason is
fastidious;
But being frugal in love is pestilent.
The light of reason is a shame for love;
Becoming old in the time of youth is bad.
O lover! Come back home;
Life without love is like dust.
Place hands on your heart;
Emigrate from your mind.

O soily body! Don't talk about the soil;
Don't say a thing but the story of the Pure Mirror.
There is an attribute of the Creator of the firmaments inside you;
Don't say a thing but the attribute of the Creator of the firmaments.

Oh God, hurrah! Your light is giving tenderness to every nymph;
With your favor, you turn fire into the water of life.

If He closes the door on you, don't leave;
With patience, He elates you to the top.

The Candle of Home

You have knocked on our door;
You are the candle of home;
Come in.
The home of the heart is yours;
You are God;
Come in.
Home is filled and lit with your light;
The soul and heart are your place;
Where are you?
Come in.
O Beloved of home and the Cause of craziness!
O One from Whom all goodness comes!
Where are you going?
Come in.

If He closes all the ways and passages on you, He will show you a secret path that no one knows about.

Tonight, the wine of the soul is continual;
Butler is the King, and the wine is strong.
The instrument for delight is perfect.
O, spirited souls! Sleeping is forbidden.

Sama[9] became a window toward your flower garden;
Lovers' ears and hearts are on this window.
Ah! The window is a huge veil;
But go; still, it is a good thing;
Don't say a thing, O pure one!

[9] Sufi dance

The Arrival of Beloved

Come here; come here;
The flower garden has bloomed.
Come here; come here;
Beloved has arrived.
Bring all souls and the world at once;
Leave it to the Sun that has drawn the sword beautifully.
Laugh at the ugly to make it cute;
Weep for that friend who has been parted from Beloved.
The whole city! Revolt;
It is rumored that the crazy are freed of the chain.
What a day! What a day!
It is like resurrection;
Whether the letter of deeds has flown over the firmament.
Play the drums and don't say a thing;
What a place for heart and reason where even the soul is stampeded!?

Didn't I tell you not to be satisfied with the image of the world?
I am the Painter of your contentment palace.
Didn't I tell you, "I am your Ocean and you are the fish?"
Don't go to the dry land;
I am the Ocean of your joy.

If you are light of heart, know where the way home is.
If you are godly, know that I am your Chief.

Didn't I tell you not to go into the trap, like birds?
Come, I am the power of your wings and flight.
Didn't I tell you, "They will ransack and demoralize you"?
I am the Fire, Pulse, and Warmth of your air.

The Happiness Day

Come, today is a feast day for us;
Henceforth, pleasure and delight will increase.
Clap and say, "Today is happiness."
The happy day is evident from the beginning.
Who could be like our Beloved in the world?
Who has seen such a feast in a hundred eras?
The sky and the Earth are full of sweetness;
In every direction, sweetness appears.
Whatever preciousness isn't here is in the heart;
Wine, if it isn't from the cup of soul, is foul.
In admiration, I had a hangover;
I didn't know Truth is our Master.
Now I relax and let my feet rest,
As I know my fortune is pulling me.

O sorrow! Even if you become as light as a
hair, I don't bear you.
This status is full of sweets; you can't do
anything.

Sadness is in a heart empty of His whim;
All sadness goes where the Nimble Beloved
isn't.
O sorrow! If you become gold and all
sweet, I will close my mouth and say,
"The worthy don't eat sweets."

You should become unconscious,
without ear or thought, so that you hear
the call: "Come back."

Toward the Heartland

I want a lover who rises every time and
causes fiery resurrections in every
direction.
I want a fiery heart that quenches hell;
A heart that stirs two hundred seas, not
running away from the waves.
Wrapping lands like wrapping a turban in
its hands;
Hanging the eternity light like a
candelabrum.
Going to battle like a lion and having a
heart like a whale;
It doesn't let anything inside, even itself,
So that Light passes the seven hundred
hearts' veils;
The call is heard from heaven, wondrous!
wondrous!
As the heart turns from the seventh sea
toward the heartland, wondrous gems are
poured from the sea onto the shore.

The conversation appeared like a cloud of dust;
Get used to being silent for some time; sober!

It is a wonder that the soul is in a prison while the prisoner has the key to their prison.

Silence is like an ocean, and talking is like a stream; the Ocean is seeking you; don't seek the stream.

Sit by the Heart

Those who have love and desire inside
their hearts, if they don't open their hearts,
there should be a reason for that.
Go and sit by the door of heart,
Because Hidden Beloved comes at dawn or
midnight.
A separated soul seeks God;
He is such a rarity; He is such an awesome
Being.
Eyes, seeing from this porch another porch,
are such a mystic!
What a sweet nickname it has!
One having that eye is the companion of
Life and is happy in death time;
As soon as they leave this world,
They will have the beauty beside them.
Though His crown on the universe is not
visible, without having a father and
mother, He has a great lineage.
Be silent; don't divulge the secrets just
anywhere;
There might be a stranger even among
kindhearted ones.

Talking about secrets before a seer is
wrong; doing so is a sign of our negligence
and fault.
Being silent before a seer is good for you;
That's why the verse of *silence* was sent
down.

It's time for us to go crazy for your chain,
Breaking the bind and becoming alienated
from everyone.
Giving our lives, not bearing the shame of
such a place anymore;
Let's set fire to our homes and go to the
tavern, like fire.

Though we are stones, in pursuing your
love, we become soft.
Though we are candles, in pursuing your
light, we become butterflies.
Though we are kings, through your beauty,
we go to the right path;
So in this sacrifice, we become sages by
your brightness.

The Joy of Your Scent

How would one talk with you while before
you, in every moment, the soul falls and
rises?
Wherever you step, a head grows from the
soil;
So how can one give up seeking you?
The day that soul flies for the joy of your
scent,
Soul and only soul knows the pleasant
scent of Friend.
Even for a moment, if my hangover for you
is less than consciousness, a hundred
laments are heard, and every hair whines.
I've emptied my heart's home to fill it with
your face;
I decrease my attachments so your love
increases more and more.
My soul is in search of Shams e Tabrizi,
Without feet, like ships, sailing in the sea.

In front of the face of the love mirror,
Let's not talk about *self*;
We are confidants of your secrets,
becoming like butterflies.

We are like reeds, and the sound inside us is from you;
We are like mountains, and the sound within us is from you.

Our wind and our being is for your call;
All our being is for your creation.
You gave the pleasure of being to nothingness;
You caused nothingness to fall in love with you.

Beloved Is Here

O people who have gone on pilgrimage!
Where are you? Where are you?
Beloved is here; come back; come back.
Beloved is your next-door neighbor,
What are you looking for in the desert?
If you see the faceless face of your
Beloved, you'll know that you are the
dignitary, house, and the Kaaba.
Ten times you've gone through the same
path to the house in Mecca;
Once, come from the house to this roof.
That house is fine; you have talked about
its signs;
However, give the address of the Dignitary
of the house.
If you have seen the garden, where is the
bouquet?
Where is the gem of the soul if you are
from the ocean of God?
Anyway; may your pain be your treasure;
Ah! The veil on your treasure is you.

This stream may drown but will kill no one;
He is the Water of life; He isn't anything
but kindness and grace.

Annihilation by itself is such a blessing;
As the help from Existence comes through
annihilation.
All hearts are worried about *nothingness*;
This isn't *nothingness* but the garden of
heaven.

The distance from you to the invisible is
thousands of years;
If you go through the heart, it is only a
step.

Whoever is in the ascendency, what sorrow would they have?
Whoever is there, what sorrow would they have?
From this side, everything is soul and life;
From this side, all is grace and munificence.

For a lifetime, you have tested your being;
Once you should try *nothingness*.

The world is renewed in every breath;
While we are unconscious of renewal and survival.

I Am a Pure Light

I've come back! I've come back! I've come from Sweetheart;
Look at me; Look at me; I have come to soothe you.
I've come happy; I've come happy; I've come free;
It took me thousands of years to speak.
I am going there; I am going there; I was at the top; I am going up;
Free me; free me; I've come here to become conscious.
I was a heavenly bird, but I became earthly; I didn't see His trap; suddenly I was caught.
I am a pure light, not a handful of mud;
Last, I am not an oyster, I came kingly.
Don't see us with your eyes but perceive us at acme;
Come there and watch us; we are light-hearted there.
I am better than four elements and seven skies;

I am the gem, coming here for a visit.
My friend has come to the bazaar, nimble and wakeful;
Otherwise, I have nothing to do in the bazaar; I am looking for him.
O Shams e Tabrizi! When will you glance at the whole world?
In the desert of annihilation, I have come soulfully but heartsick.

Truth created suffering and sorrow to give meaning to happiness.
The coverts are known by their opposites;
As Truth doesn't have any opposite, He is hidden.

This word and song have risen from thought;
You don't know where the ocean of thought is.

How many worlds are there in the thought domain?
How deep is the fathom of the thought's ocean?

The Mirror of the Soul

How close is your soul to my soul;
So close that I know whatever you think.
Friends know each other's conscience;
If I don't know my friend's conscience, I am not an honest friend.
Friend with friend,
When water is clear, it reflects the image of purity.
People are all like mirrors, reflecting my gain and loss.
If my soul does not polish the mirror every moment, it gets murky.
No mirror becomes a mystic if you scatter the soil of the earthly world on it.
Don't turn your face away from the mirror;
The mirror is saying,
"I am the refuge of your soul."
My words and I are the mirror of the soul;
The soul finds its condition in my words.
Be silent; with gesture and coquetry,
I tell the soul a thousand adventures.

If you fill your heart with any thoughts,
They will steal something from you in secret.
So, get busy with something that is better,
So that what it steals from you is inferior.

Happy ones who became like us,
All accepting and contentment;
They got attached to love and craziness,
Becoming gems of the happiness sea.
For insight, they became the moon and sun,
Their soil became like gold;
With grace and zephyr manner,
They became the sea of gems.

When the King of Love attracts you,
He separates you from all folk;
When you choose to perceive with love,
All desires are fulfilled.

I Am You

Come! Today I am out of this world;
Come! Today I am hiding from *self*.
I took a dagger and cut my attachments;
I don't belong to *self* or others.
It was a mistake not to cut my
attachments;
My soul devised without me involved.
I don't know what the fire of heart feels
like;
My tongue is burning differently.
I have seen myself in a hundred faces;
I told every face, "I am you."
As I am saying it, a hundred faces are
appearing;
Or I am not a face, without any signs.
The faces of the heart are like guests;
They come and I am their host.

If the world is full of thorns,
The heart of a lover is all flower garden.
If the firmament becomes jobless,
The world of lovers is booming.
If all be sad, the soul of a lover is tender,
happy, and cheerful.

Though lovers might seem alone,
They aren't;
In secret, they are in companionship with
Friend.
The wine of lovers spouts from the chest;
The friend of love is of mysteries.

Everyone is a messiah of a world;
Every pain is a cure in our hands.

Let's Appreciate Each Other

Come! Let's appreciate each other,
Before suddenly missing each other.
When a faithful is the mirror of another faithful,
Why should we turn our faces from the mirror?
The benevolent ones sacrificed their souls for Friend;
Why don't we recite "I am a refugee of God" and "Say, He is God" verses so that our love is protected from evil eyes?
Grudges darken friendship;
Why not let grudges go away from the heart?
Sometimes you may be pleasant after I die;
But why do we praise the dead and become enemies of life?
After my death, you will want to reconcile;
All life, we are tested by your love.
Imagine I am dead now; reconcile;
In submission, we are like the dead.

If you want to kiss my grave later,
Kiss my cheek now; we are the same.
O heart! Be silent like the dead;
For this tongue, we are accused of
existence.

Except for being in full trust and submission,
Sorrow and comfort are all traps and deceptions.

He said to one, “Don’t look at your weakness”;
Overthinking about a weakness is ingratitude.
See your power, which is from Him;
See your power as His blessing, as it is so.

Ride on love, not thinking about the path;
The horse of love is easygoing.
Although the road is uneven, with only a ride,
The horse of love transmits you to the home.

The Love Garden

Come among us; we are lovers,
Pulling you to the door of the love garden.
Reside in our home, like a shade;
We are neighbors of the Sun.
Though our souls are not visible in this world,
And though we are without sign, like the love of lovers,
Our effects are attached to you;
Like a soul, we are both hidden and visible.
Whoever you say we are,
Look higher; we are above that.
You are water but vortex and confined;
Join us;
We are a flowing flood.
We have nothing to lose,
We don't know anything but the song of nescience.

The mother of idols is the idol of your ego.

As you look at the pinnacle of the topmost sky,
Two thousand doors of grace are opened in heaven.

All the poison of religion and the world become nectar and pleasant drink by you;
In the burning chest, sadness and pain become affectionate by you.

Happiness Day

Today, I am not heartsick but happy;
I forgot all the sadness.
I am away from whoever is heartsick
whether it is my king or master.
Today, I have decided to be happy and
uncover the veil from the Moon's face.
Today, I am tender and subtle, like being
born out of tenderness.
Friend, not kissing for coquettishness,
Kissed me while I didn't know.
Last night, I dreamed a wondrous dream;
Today, I am fully satisfied with the result.
You said, "Go, you are the king."
Yes, congratulations! I am fortunate.
Without a butler and wine, I am drunk;
Without a throne and crown, I am the king.
How could imagination reach where I am?
Glory be to God, such a marvelous place I
am in.

What can the thirsty see in a dream?
Fountain, pond, and crock.
I am thirsty to join you;
When can I revolve around you?

Everything in the world attracts something;
Warmth attracts warmth, and coldness attracts coldness.

Be happy and carefree; feel safe;
I do the same with you as the rain does with the grass.

You Are the Fire

As I saw myself like a thorn, I ran away to the flower;
As I saw myself like vinegar, I mingled with sugar.
I was a bowl full of poison, I went for an antidote;
I was a cup full of sediment, I washed the cup with the Water of life;
I had a painful perception, I touched Jesus for a cure.
I saw myself to be immature, I mingled with the mature.
I found the soil of love's alley to be the kohl of the soul;
I became a strand of hair in tenderness, refining the kohl.
Love says, "You are telling the truth, but don't think it is by you";
I am the wind; you are the fire;
I awakened you.

When your heart is the house of your secrets,
Your desires will come true sooner.

When a seed is hidden inside the earth,
Its mystery turns to greenery and garden.

The promise of the munificent: a flowing treasure;
The promise of the ill-natured: a flowing pain.

The Infinite Grace

Oh, sudden resurrection! The infinite grace,
Kindling the fire in the thicket of thoughts.
Today you've come smiling, freed from jail;
For God's bounty and clemency,
You've come to the poor.
You are the veil on the Sun,
Obliged to be hopeful,
You are both the desire and aspirant;
You are the beginning and the end.
Risen in the chests, adorning the thoughts,
You desire, and you fulfill it.
Oh, the Unique Resuscitator!
You are the joy of knowledge and action.
The rest is an excuse and lie:
This is a reason or that is a remedy.
In our dishonesty, we have become
pessimistic, being in enmity with the
innocent.
Sometimes drunk with a nymph,
Sometimes drunk with bread and porridge.
See this drunkenness, let reason go;
See the sweetness, let the learned
knowledge go.

For the sake of bread and greenery, this
adventure is not worthy.
Throw your paper and break your pen;
Butler has arrived! Come.

In the fire of love, you are like Abraham;
Be happy; God saves you.

How could souls reach your Essence while they are drowned in your attributes?

He has tested you in every direction,
Pulling you toward directionlessness, so that you submit.

The Song of Happiness

O Whose light is our summer behind veils!
Take us to the garden with a warm heart, like summer.
O Who adorns the eyes of the soul, where have you gone?
Come back and pour the water of your grace on our firebox.
Come back so that dandruff turns to greenery and graves become gardens.
Come back so that grapes are sweetened and bread is baked.
O, Sun of the soul and heart! O, before Whom the Sun is embarrassed!
Look at this water and soil and bind our souls.
For the love of your face, thorns have turned into gardens many times,
Throwing a hundred thousand confessions in our faith.
O, the face of eternal love!
Toward the One, you are handsome in your body, emigrating from this prison.
In the smoke of sorrow, inaugurate happiness,

Showing the day in the absolute night.
O our Shining Dawn! On a wondrous day,
You give the kingdom to the inferior;
Be happy, O our king!
What eyes deserve you? They can't even reach your dust;
What conscious ears could hear our reason?
As the heart becomes the reservoir of goodness,
The song of happiness is heard from the heart.
Details are going back to the Origin;
Green by green, flower by flower, they are freed from the prison of thornland.

Strictness and prejudice are from immaturity.

Thoughts can't contain Who you are;
You are not the effect but the Cause.

As illusions were gone,
Your unreasonableness became clear to you.

The Victorious Fortune

O our Reputed Joseph! You are going well on our roof;
O Who has broken our cup! O Who has torn off our trap!
Oh, our Light! Oh, our Feast! Oh, our Victorious Fortune!
Thrill our passion so that our grapes turn to wine;
O Beloved and our Purpose! O Qibla and our God!
You lit a fire in our incense;
Look at our smoke.
O our Friend and Sweetheart!
The Trap of our hangover hearts;
Don't leave us;
The garden is pledged for our turbans.
Heart's foot is stuck in the mud;
I give my soul; what about the heart?
From the fire of crazy heart,
Ah, heart! Ah, us!

Why did you become miserable for a thought?
You have become depressed and sad.
I collected you together while you were in pieces;
Why are you torn apart to a hundred fragments by temptation?

You are the child of life; your job is to love.
Why have you gone, doing whatever?

O dear! Everybody mingles with their own kind;
Everyone chooses a beloved whom they deserve.
Whoever is marked for you, no one will buy;
Whoever is your prey, no one will hunt.

The Garden of Hope

Friend is mine; the Crony is mine;
lovelornness is mine;
You are my Friend; you are my Crony;
O Dignitary! Hold me.
You are Noah; you are Soul;
You are Victory; you are the Opening.
You are the opened chest of secrets.
You are the bird of Mount Sinai;
I am a bird with a tired beak!
You are the drop; you are the sea;
You are the grace; you are the wrath;
You are the sweetness; you are the poison;
Don't bother me more.
You are the chamber for the Sun;
You are the house of Venus;
You are the garden of hope; let me get in;
O Friend!
You are the day; you are the fast;
You are the water; you are the jug;
Water me this time.
You are the seed; you are the trap;
You are the wine; you are the cup;

You are the sophistication; you are the naivety; don't let me stay naive.
If I could be unselfish and my heart stay pure, I would find the path and wouldn't need to speak so much.

When you become the branch of a tree, cut from the other,
You are seeking union with this one; leave the other.

Ocean water is fully under your command;
Water and fire, O God!, are for you.
If you want, the fire turns to happiness water;
And if you don't want to, even water turns to fire.

In the sweet land of the heart,
Even a sugar cube is embarrassed;
How could you frown and be grumpy!?

Water of Life

Beloved! May you accept our quest;
We are the servants and devotees of love;
Grab our hair.
Without a butler and cup, give a wine like a tulip;
So that flower prostrates the visage of our faces.
Today, make our eyes drunk;
Make our alley one that paradise envies.
We are the mine of gold and wealth;
Who doesn't want these?
We give bliss to our friends and adversaries.
We have become the candle of style with long necks;
Warming with wine, you opened our throats.
O Water of life! You flooded us;
It is now licit; break our crock.
If you don't know our tempers, ask about the favor of wine;
Wine has made our tempers like itself.

If you pour an ocean of wine, it won't satisfy us, as you have put our cups upside down.
Groups of drunks are arriving in the garden;
A drunk smelling our fragrance, who wouldn't want to come?
Mercury, if it hears about our way,
Will leave artisticness and everything else.
Stop!
The world becomes bitter for people on the Earth if by chance they hear our dialogue.

The soil is loyal;
Whatever you sow, you'll reap the same
without any unfaithfulness.

Before His Being, one shouldn't exist.
What is existence before Him? Unpleasant.

I have tested the foresight of mind;
Henceforth, I make myself crazy.

In Longing for You

In longing for you, I am bewildered, day and night;
I won't give up even for a moment.
I make day and night crazy like me;
I won't leave day and night even for a moment.
They wanted the soul and heart of lovers;
I am surrendering my soul and heart, day and night.
Until I find what is in my thoughts, I don't lose even a moment.
As soon as your love begins the song of joy,
I am in a moment a harp, in another moment a string of musical notes.
You hit the wound and go away;
And I become lamentable until firmament, day and night.
Butler! You made a human crazy in the dawn;
I am hungover from the wine, day and night.
O Whose bridle of lovers is in your hand!
I am among lovers, day and night.

Unconscious, I am drunkenly bearing your burden,
Like a camel bearing cargo, day and night.
Let me break my fast with your sweetness;
Otherwise, I will keep fasting until the resurrection.
As I break my fast beside the table of grace,
My feast begins forever, day and night.
I swear to day and night and to your soul;
I am waiting, day and night.
I won't wait for a year for the feast to come;
With your moon, I am the feast, day and night.
Since the night you promised the day of the reunion, I have been counting days and nights, day and night.
It's enough;
My soul is thirsty for sowing love;
In the clouds of my eyes,
I am full of tears, day and night.

As you become hopeless due to loneliness;
You become a sun under the shade of Beloved.
Soon go and seek God as your Beloved;
As you do so, God is your Helper.

After that, wherever you go will be the east;
All easts will fall in love with your west.

When the mirror of the heart is pure and clean,
You see figures beyond water and soil.
You will see the painting and its Painter;
As well as the carpet of fortune and its Knitter.

Moon Stands Beside You

In the breath that you are with *self*,
Beloved seems to you like a thorn;
In the breath that you are *selfless*, Beloved
is working for your good.
In the breath that you are with *self*, you
are the prey of a mosquito;
In the breath that you are *selfless*, you are
hunting an elephant.
In the breath that you are with *self*, you
are tied to the cloud of sorrow;
In the breath that you are *selfless*, Moon
stands beside you.
In the breath that you are with *self*,
Beloved withdraws;
In the breath that you are *selfless*,
Beloved's wine is poured for you.
In the breath that you are with *self*, you
are depressed, like the autumn;
In the breath that you are *selfless*, winter
turns into spring for you.
Your disquiet is because you demand;
Be a restless seeker until constancy comes
to you.

All unpleasantness of the non-digestible is
because of trying to digest;
Withdraw digestion so that even poison
becomes salubrious.
Your desires are not fulfilled because you
demand it;
Otherwise, all your desires are given to you
like gifts.
Fall in love with Beloved's encounters, not
His affection,
So that Pampering Beloved comes to you
in love.
The king of the east and religion, Shams, if
he comes from Tabriz, I swear to God,
you'll be ashamed to look at the Moon and
stars.

For love, the earthly body is on firmament;
The mountain has begun to dance and become agile.

My eyes are adorned with the Kohl of Divine Glory;
It is the house of existence, not a home of illusion.

No asset is better than trusting in Beloved;
What is dearer than surrendering to Truth?

The Fire of Truth

If the soul of a lover blows,
It sets fire to this world,
Disarranging the baseless universe, like particles.
All the universe becomes an ocean,
The ocean becomes nothing because of awe;
A human won't be a human anymore if he mingles with Adam;
Smoke is spiking from the firmament,
Neither a human nor an angel.
The smoke suddenly sets fire to the great dome,
Splitting the sky;
At that moment, nothing remains of the world;
A rapture begins in the universe,
And the feast overcomes the mourning.
Sometimes fire wins over the water;
Sometimes water eats the fire;
Sometimes the waves of nothingness ocean take over the night and day.
The Sun fades away before the light of the human's soul;

Talk with strangers less about things that
intimates are silent about.
Mars is brave; Jupiter is burning the
evidence;
Moon is losing its majesty; its happiness
hits the sadness.
Mercury falls into the swamp; Saturn is on
fire;
Venus doesn't dare to play the happy song.
No arc remains, not even a rainbow or
wine in the cup;
No pleasure remains, not even a little joy;
No wound is healing.
Water doesn't paint nor does wind pave;
The Garden does not rejoice, and the cloud
of the canebrake doesn't rain.
No pain remains, no remedy;
No enmity remains, no witness.
Reed doesn't remain nor tune;
The harp doesn't play the pitch.
Truth has ignited a fire to burn everything
but truth.

Even for a moment or timepiece, I don't withdraw from you;
Because you are my work; because you are my fruit.

It feels like my soul and yours are one;
I swear to my only soul, I dislike everything but you.

If your thorn is like this, how would your flower garden be?
O Mystery! Your mysteries are my secrets.

The Wine of Heaven

Your thought is flowing in the river of soul like the living water;
For your love, the water of life is an explorer flowing in your river.
The bird of my heart flies as it hears the sound of birds;
For, hearing their sound, I give my life happily and smiling.
Every bird of soul has made a love collar, like a ringdove;
As *I* is freed from the cage, going toward Soliman.
Each moment, from the soul of glory, a drunk, ruined, and annihilated spiritual being ascends to the throne of glory.
What is soul? The crock of King; inside is the wine of heaven.
Hence, words are spontaneously said each moment, disheveled.
In my eating is a different gusto, in my going another gusto;
In my sayings is another gusto, and the eternity is going like this.

O Moon! With encounters between me and you, the field is happy;
Whoever has a lame horse is leaving the field lamely.
The Moon, seeking your polo, has made itself like a ball;
The Sun is also infatuated,
Moving like a rolling ball.
In such a hurry, the Moon and the Sun did not reach you, woven in your Light and moving outside the veranda.
If the outside light is like this, for those who see the fortune, O Lord! What a reverence! O Lord! What a shining move.

You are revolving around my heart; I am revolving around your door;
Revolving on your hand, I am bewildered, like a compass.

The song of your tambourine is hidden while the dance of the world is evident.

I went to a dervish; he said, "May God be your helper";
As though his prayer was accepted because a King like you is my helper.

The Heaven of Lovers

Drunkenness is greeting you, secretly
giving you the message;
Where are the ones whose hearts you have
taken? The soul is also your servant.
O Who has turned existence to inexistence!
Hear the greeting from the drunk,
A drunk who binds his two hands in your
trap.
O Heaven of lovers! O Life of lovers!
Your goodness among lovers, now, makes
happiness.
You are the flavor of every lip! The Qibla of
every religion;
The Moon revolves every night around your
roof, like a constable.
O heart! How drunk and happy you are;
you are kingly and royal.
With this gusto and disobedience, He will
tame you like love.
He is the One Who enlivens soil with a soul
and turns smoke into a galaxy.
You are the soil of the body;
He is the Smoke of heart;
Look what He will turn you to.

Ask the King for butlers, and be drunk like the rest;
If you are half drunk, you are imperfect!
Drunkenness completes you.
For your love, the Moon was split in half
and faces are heartsick;
See wailing and tearfulness in love;
Look at the maturity in work, though the wine in the cup makes you naive.
O rosy wine! Look at His generous hands;
He makes you legitimate for the soul but forbidden for the body.
So I am not a body; I am a soul; not a gem but a mine of gems;
O heart! Don't be afraid of notoriety;
He gives you honor and reputation.
Don't continue; leave the conversation;
Don't say a verse or prose;
The Devisor is inducing your words.

For zeal, I am silent;
As from your candy string, I am a sugar-scattering cloud, raining only sweetness.

From the reflection of Friend's face in this flower garden, in every way, there is a moon, a sun, and Pleiades, O God!

O God! It is for the Water of life that we are revolving, not for clapping, reed, or tambourine.

It Will Delight You

Say something new so that two worlds be renewed;
Transcending the world's limits, becoming limitless and immeasurable.
A wretch is one who didn't become fresh with your breath;
Either all become colors or all become songs.
Whoever becomes a ring of your door will soon take the trove of gold;
Especially if you open the door, they become the intimates of the gate.
How could water know that it would become a teller gem?
How could soil know that it would become a revealer of secrets?
No one's face has beauty without the help of your ruby lips.
If their faces are beautiful without you, it is due to using magenta dye.
Saleh's camel[10] was born from the mountain;
I am sure; the mountain became an agile camel hearing your good news.
Keep the secret; be silent, though being silent might not be easy;

---

[10] Saleh, a prophet mentioned in the Quran, summoned his people to a mountain, where they witnessed the rock miraculously split open, revealing the camel.

What seems sorrowful will delight you.
Bring any poison to Him so that He turns it to better than sugar;
Present wrath before Him so that He turns all to contentment.

In two worlds, where is a king tenderer and happier than our King?
His eyebrows didn't frown, though He saw a hundred faults.

Don't go far away; don't go on a journey; your Moon is beside you;
Don't shout! He is listening to the whisper of your prayer.

Let Friend Come In

Wash the path promptly;
Beloved is arriving.
Give good news to the garden;
The fragrance of spring is smelled.
Let Friend come in, the Full Moon;
From His shining face, the gift of his light is scattering.
The sky is cracked, a ruckus in the universe;
Amber and musk are blowing;
The flag of Beloved is arriving.
The boom of the garden is arriving;
Sweetheart is coming;
The arrow is going toward the target.
Why are we seated? King is coming back from hunting;
The garden greets; the cedar stands up.
The green is going on foot; the Rider Bud is arriving;
Hermits of heaven are drinking wine;
The soul is drunk and ruined; the intellect is hungover.
As you arrive in our alley, you'll know that silence is our manner.
From this conversation arises a cloud of dust.

If it wasn't for His word, how would your soul sigh? Sigh so that your sigh leads you toward God.

The eyes get drunk from the nectar of His eyes;
The trees dance before the tenderness of Zephyr.

The needle hole of whim is tight; believe it;
He doesn't let anyone grab His rope if they see Him in duality.

The Immortal Light

I want a love such that every time it rises
fiery resurrections arise in every direction.
I want a heart like hell to quench the hell,
Disquieting two hundred seas but not
running away from sea waves.
Wrapping territories like a turban by its
hands,
Hanging the immortal light like a
candelabrum.
If a lion comes in a battle, that heart
appears to be a whale,
Not letting anything be but itself yet
challenging itself.
When the heart passes the seven hundred
veils of itself by its light,
A call is heard from the throne of heaven:
Bravo, Bravo.
When arriving by the mountain Qaf[11] after
passing the seventh sea,
What gems it pours from the sea onto the
soil!

---

[11] Mount Qaf is a legendary mountain in the popular mythology of the Middle East.

For the love's hand, every hand becomes a court of granting;
From you, the disloyal world becomes a loyalty workshop.

What happens to a heart when holding the hands of a beloved?

Beloved loves this disquietude;
A vain endeavor is better than sleeping.

Our origin is angel-born, deserving to always be happy.

Don’t despond; cheer yourself up; shout out before the Savior.

Know your value is whatever you waver for;
That’s why the value of a lover’s heart is more than the heavenly throne.

A Pearl Inside You

One having you, why shouldn't they be
happy?
One seeing you, O Moon!, what sorrow
would they have?
For your crystal color, your nuisance is
sweet;
Although your nuisance is quite short-lived.
O from Whom the coquettishness of nymph
arises!
O from Whom the shining of light comes!
O Who has two hundred students and
retinues like the Moon!
You are Sun without any retinues;
Though the retinues of your goodness have
a hundred drums and flags.
Under the shade of your curvy plaits,
Many infatuated lovers are relaxed and
well-slept.
I said, "O my Beloved! Don't break me with
your nuisance."
He said, "You are like an oyster with a
pearl inside you."
O infatuated! Unless you aren't broken, the
pearl won't be evident;
A pearl that is inside my idol, or it is my
idol.

How would the phoenix of a lover's heart fit in a trap? The flight of such a bird is beyond this universe!

Each moment, in sorrow or ease, is a cunning trap; trust and fully submit.

Hurrah God! Hurrah God! You freed me abruptly from sadness.

In Your Happiness Garden

O, love! Are you more elegant
Or is your garden and apple orchard more so?
O, Moon! Whirl to enliven enthusiasts.
With you,
Bitterness turns into sweetness,
Disbelief and deviation become the right path,
Dust becomes a flower.
You placed gates in the skies,
And feathers onto humans.
O, Love! How sweet is your manner!
How pretty is your face!
How you adore mirth.
Happiness is your peer.
Your color is on all flowers,
All truths are from you.
Every particle is in your melody longing for your beneficence.
All bazaars are withered without you,
The gardens and flowers ask for your rain.
The trees learn to dance thanks to you,
The branches exult with you.
The leaves get drunk on your living stream.

If the garden wants a new spring,
It scatters its leaves on your flower bestrewing breeze.
How pleasant your calling is in your happiness garden,
Whoever your guest is eats happiness instead of food!
I have tried for some time without you,
Without you, I have no joy.
How would life be enjoyable without your unending sweetness?
No plan devising benefited me,
But my heart unshackled the chains,
Dragging my spirit before your lively Soul.
O, To whom the mountain is embarrassed and heart is bold in virtue of your forbearance!
The perky heart jumps on your veranda.
You open countless knots in arduous situations,
And my heart, like an ant, is searching for a narrow breach to enter your sea.
If I try to count your bounty and describe your face before the resurrection, I can't do so.
How can I pass your sea whilst being tipsy?

From Him you will find all your desires fulfilled; He makes you both drunk and sober.

What is our desire? His strong, heady wine; What is the wish of our hearts? His everlasting grace.

Don’t argue; ask for the felicity of love.

Happy Your Freedom

O heart! You have fallen in love;
Happy being enthusiastic!
You have left the place here;
Happy being there!
Condone both worlds; play the song and drink alone,
So that the unseen realm says,
“Happy your freedom.”
O leader of humanity!
Today you are bearing;
O ascetic of tomorrow!
May your tomorrow be blessed.
All your disbelief turned to belief;
All your bitterness turned to sweetness;
You have become all sweet;
Happy sweetness!
In the house of the chest, there is a tumult for the dervish;
O hateless chest! Happy breakthrough!
This eye, perceiving the heart, was a tear, becoming an ocean;
Its ocean is constantly saying,
“Happy becoming an ocean!”

O secretive lover! May Beloved be your companion;
O seeker of upwardness! Happy progress!
O admirable soul! Seeking and trying!
Your feathers have grown!
Happy feathers!
Be silent; keep it secret;
You’ve made a great deal;
What merchandise you’ve got!
Happy merchandise!

You have tied our being to absolute annihilation and the fulfillment of our desires to the condition of not wanting.

Don’t be sad about decreasing;
Like the Moon, you will increase after decreasing.

Asking God for anything other than God is an illusion of increase while it is a big loss.

Infatuated With Him

O friend! Is sugar better or
Is the One Who makes the sugar?
Is the goodness of the Moon better or the One Who makes the Moon?
Oh! Is your garden better or the flower garden in you or the One Who makes the flower, creating a hundred fresh amaryllis?
Is your mind better in knowledge and insight or the One Who creates in each moment a hundred pieces of wisdom and insights?
O love! Though you are tumultuary and clamorous,
There is something in the fire that is the backbone of love.
I am infatuated with Him, bewildered and wandering;
Sometimes my feathers are burned, and other times He makes new feathers.
For His favor, the ocean of love is full of lovers and beloveds;
From the drop of thought, He makes a hundred gems.

All the gems have been broken in love,
And from the wondrous love, He makes something new.
Shams e Tabrizi's truth is making from our hearts in action a sword but in essence a shield.

Whoever is in search of being free from *self* is doing fabulous work; a hundred joys are within a soul freed from *self*.

Don't be scared even if a thousand locks are on your heart; ask for the store of heart-opening love.

I am a candle for earthly beings and a light for heaven; I am the soul for angels and a being for stars.

You Are My Life

Sweetheart! Abandon the misery;
Magnanimity doesn't approve the misery;
Look at a pain that no one has a cure for.
My basin fell from the firmament,
And I drowned in the ocean;
Inside the ocean, my heart was not
familiar with anything but you.
I just received hot news from Zephyr;
I swear to my yellowish face and your
Pretty Being,
One's heart is charmed by gold if one
doesn't have a beloved like you.
O Butler! Slow down;
Close the interior door;
Tell anyone coming to the door,
"Don't enter the mystery room."
All my life I haven't been so happy and
cheerful like this;
In loyalty to Beloved, Whose own heart
isn't loyal,
What is better than this happiness, that
you are my life and world?

Why are lovers sorrowful?
The world is passing.
Let's get drunk tonight for the charm of Beloved's sweet lips;
No one turns away from us taking off our clothes, as no one has worn a cloak.
On the day of the reunion with Beloved, all soil turns to gold;
Though the Pretty Face does so without an alchemical oven.
Insensible eyes become lightful with the beauty of Beloved,
Though the dust of His alley does so without any panacea.
Beware! I become silent;
Give my prayer and sincerity;
What can one do who doesn't have anything but prayer?

Though I appear like a particle, I am a sun; though I may seem like a detail, I am the entire being.

Thank God for opening the knots;
As we committed to an attitude of gratitude, He opened our knots.

The harm hits the oyster, not the gem.

The Heart Is Pointing to Him

A Grass in Whom all flowers take refuge;
A Grass without autumn where no flowers fall down.
A happy, cheery Tree in the middle of the desert;
Where anyone sleeping under His shade wakes up drunk.
A Firmament like the heavens Who is the soul's destination;
Where Saturn does not come even close to Venus to challenge;
You are a tender gem, in a place of placelessness;
As eyes are weeping, the heart is pointing to Him.

The purity of the mirror describes the beauty of the heart; a heart that can contain the face of Infinity.

Until you are looking for a gem, you are a gem. Until you are in caprice for a piece of bread, you are a piece of bread.
You are wise if you know this point:
You are what you are looking for.

A thousand clouds of favor are in the sky of contentment; if I rain, I will rain on you from that cloud.

You Are the Best

I've tried everything; I didn't find anything better than you;
As I dived into the ocean, I didn't find any gem better than you.
I opened many crocks, drinking from a thousand jars;
None made my lips and head as happy as your unfailing wine.
How could the flower and jasmine not smile in my heart as an elegant Beloved like you is by my side?
For a few days, in pursuing you, I gave up my wanting;
What wanting would I have if my Facilitator didn't come?
For a few days, I became the servant of your kingship;
Then there wasn't any king who wouldn't be my servant.
As the bird of my heart flew from my body toward your roof,
I whined like a nightingale about why my bird didn't come back.

For pursuing the bird of heart, I flew like a falcon;
No bird would be my peer.
Go away, O heartsick body and regretful heart!
Unless I free myself from both of you, I won't get a new heart.

The Desire of Desire

Heart's tune is playing the song;
Venus also has started the melody since dawn;
Good tidings! The happy musician is playing happy songs.
Ocean gives generously;
Remove the earplugs from your ears;
Last night, He gave us shoes and gave you the nectar.
Love is the auspicious foundation; the sermon is in its name;
May the shade of the King forever be on us.
His pretty face is like a spark; His good temper is like a new spring;
Besides all these, He is Lord of His servants.
Since the very first day, this hangover made me restless; your stormy love is pulling me like a cloud.
Heart abandoned the suffering; though the drunk Sweetheart knotted the hair, He opened the other one.
He is pulling me; I am wandering and sullen;

But go anyway; the Desire of the universe
is pulling me without my will.
Intellect reasons; coquettishness caresses.
Because of hesitancy, my feet were stuck
in the mud;
Thankfully, I am certain now.
I tear off this rope; I will return to the tryst;
I said, “Who are you?” He said, “The Desire
of all.”
I said, “Who am I?” He said, “The desire of
Desire.”
As I began to talk with the Essence, my
heart disappeared.

Unless you get drunk with God,
Sadness doesn't separate from you;
Unless you go towards the ocean,
You won't find gems and coral;
Unless you root out the thorn of sadness,
You won't obtain the flower of the garden.

Let flow the water of love life in our veins;
Tell the tale of dawn at night.
O, Initiator of new hilarity!
Move in the vein of our soul!
Be the orrery cup of the universe and the shore of the two worlds.

Lovers are apparent but Beloved is unseen.
Who has seen such love in the entire universe?

In the Realm of Love

With Love, I have reached somewhere
even love doesn't know;
The Affair has come to a place where even
reasoning is staring.
If the mind is blocked here, what could be
an opening?
O heart! Are you drunk to rely on the mind?
In the realm of love, the mind has no place
to sit; how could it help you to sit?
Mind's commodity is evidence while love is
soul-stirring and gives the soul in spiritual
encounters.
If you have woven a thousand souls,
hearts, and wisdom together,
Without love you can't reach the peephole.
You won't see the face of Beloved but
through the trap of His plait;
However, attempt to get more experience.
Though you might be a falcon, your eyes
are covered; uncovering your eyes is in His
hands;
Yet He might make you run to every alley
like a partridge.

Whoever has a pillow from the court of Divine knowledge, I am their servant even when they are sleeping.
When a lion's heart aims at a gazelle, a thousand gazelles are saved from that lion.
When a bird is aimed at by the bow of an archer, a thousand captured birds are freed from the trap.

If the world continues for thousands of centuries and I am gone, among lovers, I will be the legend of their nights.

When my sigh reached heaven, my tears fell on the soil;
I am not from here, I have lost my nest.

Don't go, but if you go, take my soul with you. And if you don't take me with you, don't go.

Saying *Hi* to the Heart

One night, I made a heart circle in the
caprice of saying *hi* to the heart;
A voice was heard: "Who is it?" I said, "It's
me, the servant of the heart."
The flame of Moon's light shone from the
door orifice;
On the passerby's heart and eyes, by the
good name of heart.
In the light of heart face, waves have filled
the heart's alley;
The pot of the Sun and Moon has become
humble before the cup of heart.
Though the all-wise patronizes, it is a
servant of the heart;
Intellect is helpless, and a hundred like
that are tied to the trap of the heart.
Light is getting from Him the throne and
great empyrean;
Soul, sitting by His door, is looking at the
roof of the heart.
All beings are drunk with the heart and
humble before it.
The stages of the nine firmaments are only
two steps away through the heart.

Who is a particle to say, “O Sun, don’t go”;
Who is a servant to say, “O King, don’t go.”
But you are the Water of life, and all creatures are fish;
However, for the sake of your generosity, kindness, and grace, don’t go!

Today I smelled your scent in the wind;
In gratitude, I gave my heart to the wind.

Dance drunkenly before our Moon,
O musician! For God’s sake, play the lovelorn melody.

My Heart Is Soft

I am unconscious, but I want to be more unconscious than this;
I am talking to your eyes, saying, “I want to be so drunk.”
I don’t want a crown; I don’t want a throne;
I want to fall on the earth and serve you.
My Good Friend grabbed my collar, asking me, “What do you want?”
I said, “I want what you are doing now.”
I want to talk with Zephyr,
But I have my own language; I want a great confidant.
The circle of my sanctuary is safe from my harm;
In pursuing your signet ring, my heart is soft because I want the pattern of the ring gem.
O heart! Inside the heart of the moon there is another moon hidden;
I am sure about it; surely I want it.

I have driven away the wave; I am outside the Ocean; I will drum all the way to the shore of your arms.

Tonight, I am your guest;
My hands and your lap.
Either you open the door lock,
Or I play the tambourine until dawn.

O for Whom my wisdom is His prey!
Shooting is your motto.
Touch my heart's thumb with your hand
and aim for my soul.

The Image of Beloved

Today, O Moon! We aren't strangers;
We are so drunk that we don't know the way home.
In your love, we are freed from reason's predicament;
We don't know any feelings but craziness and frenzy.
In the garden, we don't see anything but the image of Beloved;
We don't know anything about the branches but their drunken state.
They said, "Someone has placed a seed in this trap";
We are so drunk in the trap that we don't care about the seed.
Today, don't talk about the seed and fairy tale;
Our hearts don't accept any myth, nor do we know any.
Like a comb, our hearts have entered the plaits such that we are unconscious, not discerning the comb and hair.
Pour the wine; don't ask, "How many cups have you drunk?"
With your thought, we don't discern the cup and wine.

O to Whom my heart and soul are
servants!
Your laugh is the candy string!
Say what your laugh is for,
O, Effervescence of the Munificent Ocean!

Up to when we didn't prostrate on the soil of the Friend's door, we didn't have peace of mind in this wandering.

You shouldn't say, “We don't have a way to
the King.”
Working with mercifuls is not difficult.

Reconcile Now

Let's appreciate one another so that we
aren't unaware of one another.
As a faithful is for sure the mirror of
another faithful,
Why do we turn away from the mirror?
Benevolents have sacrificed their souls for
Friend;
Let hatred go; we are humans.
Grudge darkens friendship;
Why don't we drive away grudges from our
hearts?
Then you become good-hearted about my
going;
Why are we dead worshipers and enemies
of life?
Because after death, will you reconcile?
All our lives, we have undertaken a test for
your love.
Think I am dead now; reconcile now;
In submission, we are like the dead.
If you want to kiss my grave later, kiss my
face now; we are the same now.
Be silent like the dead,
As we are accused of existence for this
tongue.

An alive love in the soul and eye is,
at each moment, fresher than a bud.

This world is like a mountain and our
actions are like a call;
The sound of every call comes back to us.

I have come to blazon you in this house,
Raising you, like the prayer of lovers,
beyond the firmament.

We Are Happy

We are alive for the light of Greatness and Glory;
We are strangers yet are very familiar.
If we show our faces to the Moon,
It will repent of its conceit.
If we open our wings and feathers,
Sun's wings and feathers will burn.
The body of a human is only a cover;
We are the Qibla of all prostrations.
See the Divine's soul within, not a human;
So that your soul, with grace, reaches sublimity.
Devil perceived two, thinking we are separate from Truth.
We are happy, as we deserve King.

At the time,
I fell to the bottom of an ocean,
a moment later,
I rose like the Sun.

I am a portraitist and painter, making an idol in each moment;
Then I melt all the idols before you.
I stimulate a hundred figures and fuse them in my soul; as soon as I see you,
I throw them in the fire.

Through your grace, I became life and hidden from self. O, Whose Being is hidden in my hidden being!

The Broken Repentance

O Who has broken my repentance! Where can I run away from you?
O Who is sitting in my heart! Where can I run away from you?
O Who is the light of my eyes! How can I see without you?
You have tied my neck; where can I run away from you?
From your light, the six directions are like mirrors;
Your face is auspicious; where can I run away from you?
The soul is tired; where can I run away from you?
Even if I close my eyes and annul my perception,
You aren't disconnected from my heart;
Where can I run away from you?

I fly to seven skies and pass seven oceans; if you see me lovingly, you sense my wandering soul.

As soon as you came beside me, belief and disbelief became my servant. O, seeing you is my religion and your face is my faith!

One moment you give me pain; in another moment you bring me to the garden; you pull me towards the light so that my eyes open to see.

As our home is not soil, if the body pours on the soil, it doesn't matter.
My aim is not the firmaments,
O Whose reunion is my universe!

Don't look for me in this world and hereafter;
I am in a world in which these two worlds are lost!

The Harp Is Roaring

In caprice of meeting you, the stone is split;
In the delight of your desire, the wings of the soul are flapping.
Fire becomes water; reason is ruined;
Enemy falls asleep; my eyes belong to you.
The vesture of patience is torn off; reason is gone;
I died; your dragon-like love eats stone.
Don't tie the goer; don't turn laughing into crying;
Don't oppress; your servant has nothing else to replace you with.
What is the food for your love? My burning heart;
What is my ruined heart? The workshop of your loyalty.
The crock is boiling; who is drinking from it?
The harp is roaring in praising your attributes.
Love entered my door, putting its hand on my head and seeing me without you, and said, "Woe!"
It is a challenging home to stay in, dramatic and complex;
I left while a heart killed by you stayed with me.

The Inner Loyalty

Lo! Lovers! Good news! This separation won't last;
Reunion felicity is within reach; God is going to be the Deity.
Abundance will come from munificence;
Two thousand feasts will come;
Two worlds will come like devotees, yet where are you?
Sowing the sweetness of loyalty and being like soul's smoke, you abash the time, rising in the ninth firmament.
Your generosity is a magnet fulfilling the heart's desire; no sorrow here and hereafter remains, Happiness gives happiness.
Lo! Honest lovers! Don't go without accordance;
The preceding bliss was for the inner loyalty.
You were soil; behold! You began an inner journey and became a human; you won't stay in this state.
Begin your journey to heaven, move step by step, and let God free you.

Look at the drop of blood; you called it a heart moving around the universe without a wing or foot.
In a breath toward the west, in another breath toward the east, and in the next breath toward the throne and heaven, you are from the light of friends.
Look at the light of eyes touching the skies;
Show Familiar to those whom He has blessed with light.
Be silent in speaking; can't you take a step?
If you are honorable, why are you held captive in the impasse?

Seeing beauty is a condition of being a human; don't look for fault in others.

Asleep or awakened, I am thirsty for Beloved. I am a companion and paired with His imagination.

Don't avow your tears for the sadness of the world.

Your King Is Merciful

O Beloved! Like fire, you have a continual chalice;
In response to every greeting, you have a cup.
If the soul gives two thousand lives for you,
God reveals, "You are still in debt."
As I heard your greeting, I said goodbye to the comfort;
O Beloved! You have a thousand fires in your greeting.
In serving you, kings' lives were burnt;
How could I say that you have a servant like me?
As I say your attribute, my heart wavers;
O heart! Don't be scared; your King is merciful.

Don’t interpret love without wisdom.
If you don’t have a gem in your hand,
don’t open your palm.
If you don’t know color science, don’t
divide flowers into categories of beautiful
and ugly.

The confession candle kindles the heart.

Even if there are thousands of traps on the path, as you are with us, we don’t have any sorrow.

Weep Like Rain

Last night, I made my recourse to Him,
saying, “O Gift Gem!
Good night! Don’t talk, nor be picky;
Tonight you are ours.”
His charming face shone like a reddish
star, and He said, “Stop; withdraw; until
when are you going to beg?”
I said, “The Messenger of Truth said, ‘Ask
your desire from the Pretty Face until it is
fulfilled.
The Pretty Face is moody and willful
because His coquettishness and pickiness
go well together.’”
I said, “If it is so, His pickiness is the life of
the soul; as the talisman works whenever
you try it.”
He said, “This is a naive story; what pretty
face?
This colorful figure is a trap; this is
deception and disloyalty.”
I said, “O Good Beloved! Turn the
nothingness to existence;
Turn our copper to gold; you are the Soul
of alchemy.”

Copper should submit to find alchemy;
You are wheat but are outside the mill.
He said, “You are ungrateful; you don’t know copper; you are in doubt and comparison.”
I began to cry, saying while weeping, “You are right!”
O Origin of lightning! Come to help.
As He saw my tears, He began to laugh;
The west and east were revived with His familiar grace.
O friends and entourages! Weep like rain so that in the grass the pretties bring Beauty.

They said, “It is not found; we have looked for it”;
He said, “I long for what is not found.”

We don’t have the sorrow of hell or the greed for paradise; uncover your face because we are longing to meet you.

We are happy with the cupless wine; every morning we shine and every evening we are happy.

You Are My Moon

O Who has taken my liberty! You are our liberty;
I am the stigmas of a saffron flower; you are our tulip field.
I said, “Your lovelornness has killed me”;
He said, “What daring!”
Lovelornness doesn’t know that you are our Beloved.
I am the garden, burnt by autumn;
Make my garden laugh, as you are our Spring.
He said, “You are the harp for my melody;
What is your wailing for? You are beside Me.”
I said, “Every thought gives me a headache”;
He said, “Cut out those thoughts; you are my sword.”
I grabbed my head, showing I was hungover;
He said, “Why are you hungover? Isn’t it for Me?”
I said, “Like a spinning wheel, I swear to God, I am restless.”

He said, “Why are you restless? Isn’t it for Me?”
I talked about His sweet lips;
He sighed, meaning: Keep the secret, as you are my confidant.
O nightingale of dawn!
Greet us occasionally.
You are our fellow traveler.
You are the bird of heaven, not an earthly bird;
You are the hunt of the hereafter in our meadow.
Annihilated from self and coming into existence from Friend,
You are the light of the Creator and Creative.
You were born from water and mud and fell into fire;
Perceive loss and gain as the same, as you are my moon.
Here duality can’t be; what is Me and you?
See Me and you as One, as you are with me.
Be silent! Every pithy word has a soul;
Don’t give your soul to anybody, as you are my devotee.

The dance of my ear is your name; the
dance of my consciousness is your cup.
Make me again, I swear to your soul,
I am ruined.

Master! In the monastery and in the
mosque, I mean you.
Wherever you turn, I swear to your soul,
I turn toward you.

I don't want the fleeting life,
You are my Dear Life.
I don't want the sorrowful soul,
I swear to your soul,
You are my soul.

Anyone who has smelled the scent of your union flower does not stop dancing until sitting in your flower garden.

In a thousand ways, the soul learns courtesy from love, a courtesy that no school can teach.

O pleasant wind coming from Beloved's meadow! Pass through me because I long for the fragrance of the flower garden.

Famous Among Lovers

Captivated, I fell in love with Lively Beloved;
I am not a demon or a nymph; I am hidden from all.
I was snow, melted, and fell on the earth;
I became the smoke of heart,
Heading toward heaven.
I am not from spirits; I beware souls;
However; a soul shouldn't beware another soul;
What is the reason to beware another? I am a soul.
I reckoned One Who no one else thought of;
In the reckoning, eventually, I became so.
As I became selfless, my heart approved;
After losing control of my heart, I became what my heart said to be.
All my whines aren't from me but are His;
With the help of His lips' wine, I am infatuated and speechless.
He said, "Now that you have fallen in love with Me, why do you hide your love?"
For this word, I became famous among lovers.
For your love, I have lost my soul and world;
What am I doing in the world?
As I am done with here.

Praising you is truly praising ourselves;
As the Sun praises the praise of its eye.

As I saw your Being, in embarrassment, I became nothing.
From the love of nothing, the world of the soul came into existence.

Don't let anything enter your heart but His love; don't devise in vain;
Don't settle in your mind; sometimes, settle in your heart.

The Answers Are All *Yes*

Will this door eventually be opened? Yes.
Will Pretty Beloved show up? Yes.
Will our Butler remember drunks again with wine and cup? Yes.
Will the beauty of the new spring come toward the garden and make the fresh branches bloom? Yes.
Will it green the arches with grass and pair rose with lily? Yes.
Will the dusty, chaffy Earth be filled with musk and amber scents? Yes.
Will silver and gold mingle together? Yes.
Will this head-worshiping thought be drunk with the rosy wine? Yes.
Will weeping, mourning eyes be lightened with that visage? Yes.
Will ears, ringed to His ear, get earrings from the Goldsmith? Yes.
When the soul witness testifies, will the disbeliever's heart become a believer's heart? Yes.

As the shine of love arrives from the firmament, will the Jesus of the soul be free? Yes.
All beings are in the One; is He better than a hundred universes? Yes.
I become silent, but will in my heart forever grow cane sugar and sweets? Yes.

Patience has flown away from my heart;
Reasoning has run away from my head;
Up to where will your relentless
drunkenness pull me?

From the moonlight, night sees itself
bright;
I am a night; you are my Moon;
Don't go to the sky without me.

In each moment and at every hour, He
gives a new way, sweeter and rarer than
His previous ways.

More Poetry Collections from the Peace and Love Institute

The Garden of Rumi's Poetry
A Collection of the Best Poems of Rumi

The Garden of Hafiz's Poetry
A Collection of the Best Poems of Hafiz

The Garden of Persian Poetry
A Glance at 1,000 Years of
Persian Literature

The Art of a Loving Relationship

An Enlightening Book on Relationships for Women and Men to Master Love and Mindful Connections

Visit the *Peace and Love Institute* website at:

https://www.PeaceAndLoveInstitute.com

Printed in Great Britain
by Amazon

8487fefa-4042-4d80-837f-131f9bc57f1eR01